Diana Cao writes the kind of poetry in which the language embraces the world with craft and skill, the kind of poetry in which the relationship between line-break and sentence carries meanings of its own, the kind of poetry where the relationship between people comes more vividly via image and cadence. Which is to say: Diana Cao is a real poet, not just someone who has interesting things to say and so they arrange prose into line-breaks. Diana Cao says interesting things in a way that is memorable, she can shift tonalities so that the story goes deeper, she can repeat a line so that echo revels a new meaning. Which is to repeat: Diana Cao is a real poet. It is a joy to have this debut in my hands and to share it with you.

—*Ilya Kaminsky, author of* Deaf Republic *and* Dancing in Odessa

Diana Cao's *Slipstream* is a beautiful book about home, a missing home, a shifting home, about language, the liminal spaces between language, the pandemic, family, love, and coming of age. The speaker in these poems is questioning in declaratives and questions, "healthily troubling" through life, a speaker of this decade—thoughtful, cynical but true, troubled yet hopeful. In these poems the speaker observes the world, passes people, as people pass other people. Formally astute, constantly querying and requerying, these poems are trying to make sense of a nonsensical world.

—*Victoria Chang, author of* Obit *and* With My Back to the World

Diana Cao's *Slipstream* is marvelously and expertly imagined, rendered, sculpted from every scale of life. Her speakers lament a humble discontinued soap and take comfort in the panorama of dead stars. A stepping stone disappears as soon as the step is taken, and days drag behind our speaker like a weighted blanket. Mothers are car thieves and terrors while fathers want to exit their own pasts and decisions. I can barely keep up with the onslaught of arresting and fantastical imagery: A dawning in the two red eyes of a nocturnal insect. The compost of recently deceased for the orchard of Paradise, teeming with life. We move from Baltimore to Shanghai, from the underworld to a hospital. Truly, one of the most original minds I've seen at work in a long time.

—*Megan Fernandes, author of* I Do Everything I'm Told *and* Good Boys

In poems that stain the moon with shadows and ask "Who are you responsible for keeping alive?" Diana Cao brings forward an artful new collection that is both lyrical and urgent. These are finely made poems, and *Slipstream* is a notable debut by a formidable poet.

—*Matthew Olzmann, author of* Mezzanines *and* Constellation Route

PREVIOUS WINNERS OF THE BERKSHIRE PRIZE TUPELO PRESS FIRST / SECOND BOOK AWARD

Jalousie Allyson Paty
Selected by Diana Khoi Nguyen

Green Island Liz Countryman
Selected by Julie Carr

then telling be the antidote Xiao Yue Shan
Selected by Victoria Chang

The Air in the Air Behind It Brandon Rushton
Selected by Bin Ramke

The Many Deaths of Inocencio Rodriguez Iliana Rocha
Selected by Oliver de la Paz

Ashore Laurel Nakanishi
Selected by Carl Phillips

Fablesque Anna Maria Hong
Selected by Aimee Nezhukumatathil

Medusa Reads La Negra's Palm Elizabeth Acevedo
Selected by Gabrielle Calvocoressi

Fire Season Patrick Coleman
Selected by Carol Frost

Marvels of the Invisible Jenny Molberg
Selected by Jeffrey Harrison

Yes, Thorn Amy Munson
Selected by Paisley Rekdal

Halve Kristina Jipson
Selected by Dan Beachy Quick

Lantern Puzzle Ye Chun
Selected by D.A. Powell

Mary & the Giant Mechanism Mary Molinary
Selected by Carol Ann Davis and Jeffrey Levine

Manoleria Daniel Khalastchi
Selected by Carol Ann Davis and Jeffrey Levine

The Forest of Sure Things Megan Snyder-Camp
Selected by Carol Ann Davis and Jeffrey Levine

Flinch of Song Jennifer Militello
Selected by Carol Ann Davis and Jeffrey Levine

Cloisters Kristin Bock
Selected by David St. John

When the Eye Forms Dwaine Rieves
Selected by Carolyn Forché

Bellini in Istanbul Lilias Bever
Selected by Michael Collier

Everyone Coming Toward You David Petruzelli
Selected by Campbell McGrath

Devoted Creatures Bill Van Every
Selected by Thomas Lux

Miracle Fruit Aimee Nezhukumatathil
Selected by Gregory Orr

The Next Ancient World Jennifer Michael Hecht
Selected by Janet Holmes

WINNER OF THE 2024 BERKSHIRE PRIZE FOR A FIRST OR SECOND BOOK OF POETRY

Slipstream by Diana Cao

"I'm so glad that you will get to have the same experience I did—reading *Slipstream* for the first time and realizing, with a smile, that you're in good hands. *Slipstream* moves effortlessly between so many registers—and is a beautiful and deft mix of tradition, structure and modernity. And you will learn about the connection between ancient Chinese tales and moon landers. Few books are this engaged with our daily interactions with robots. I love the way *Slipstream* both acknowledges the ubiquity of being online and reminds us just how dumb it all really is. Throughout this book, no matter what the subject, the language is elegant and straightforward and clear; in a word, it's beautiful.

She has a way of writing about herself while using the language and worldview of the ancients. There's even a sestina that's actually good—we all know the form is too bossy and they never really work. But there's a sestina here that's loose with the rules, and so it flows; it's a triumph.

Sestinas, villanelles, a crown of sonnets, linked verse: the way the old forms are made to feel spoken and modern is a delight. This whole book is a delight. Even with the impressive range of subjects and positionalities here, the book ends with a quiet intimacy that will have you sitting up and paying attention, sad to have it end."

—Matthew Rohrer, judge for the 2024 Berkshire Prize

Diana Cao is the author of *Slipstream* (Tupelo Press, 2026), winner of the Berkshire Prize. She is also the author of the chapbook *Relational* (Sixth Finch, 2024). Her work has appeared in *Ploughshares*, *The Kenyon Review*, *The Yale Review*, *The Threepenny Review*, and elsewhere. She has received support from MacDowell, the Bread Loaf Writers' Conference, and Just Buffalo Literary Center.

SLIPSTREAM

Diana Cao

Tupelo Press
North Adams, Massachusetts

Slipstream

Library of Congress Cataloging-in-Publication Data
Names: Cao, Diana, 1990- author
Title: Slipstream : poems / Diana Cao.
Identifiers: LCCN 2025053102 (print) | LCCN 2025053103 (ebook) | ISBN 9781961209619 paperback | ISBN 9781961209626 ebook other
Subjects: LCGFT: Poetry
Classification: LCC PS3603.A63758 S56 202 (print) | LCC PS3603.A63758 (ebook)
LC record available at https://lccn.loc.gov/2025053102
LC ebook record available at https://lccn.loc.gov/2025053103

Cover and text design by Allison O'Keefe.
Front cover: Adriaen Coorte (Dutch, 1660–1707). Gooseberries on a Table. 1701. Oil on paper mounted on wood. 29.7 x 22.8 cm.
Leonard C. Hanna, Jr. Fund 1987.32 https://www.clevelandart.org/art/1987.32
Back cover: Cao, Miaofu. Diana Cao, crabbing at Sandy Point State Park. 1996. Author's personal collection.

First paperback edition August 2026

Tupelo Press
P.O. Box 1767
North Adams, Massachusetts 01247
(413) 664-9611 / Fax: (413) 664-9711
editor@tupelopress.org / www.tupelopress.org

Tupelo Press is an award-winning independent literary press that publishes fine fiction, non-fiction, and poetry in books that are a joy to hold as well as read. Tupelo Press is a registered 501(c)(3) nonprofit organization, and we rely on public support to carry out our mission of publishing extraordinary work that may be outside the realm of the large commercial publishers. Financial donations are welcome and are tax deductible.

SLIPSTREAM

to our stranger selves

CONTENTS

I

Every Day the World

arranges itself. Light breaks on courtyards
where flowers bloom into bananas and a stray cat
poses for the camera. On this evening,
we ride a carriage to Djemaa El-Fna,

where we're linguistically immune to the charms
of snake charmers and storytellers
lining the souk in a glowing overlay
of geometric cutouts, an open-air

market square we observe from a cafe.
Above tajine d'agneau and sweet mint tea,
our parents are almost content tonight,
and even my sister's willing to joke.

When Mohammed says he's never guided
a proper Chinese family before,
she says, We're not very proper. True.
Mohammed explains how the city lies

beneath the snow-capped range of the Atlas,
which melts to provide this desert with water,
and where we underestimate the climb;
my mother has worn the wrong kind of shoes.

My dad almost refuses to climb down:
afraid of heights, he won't drive on bridges
at home, or when he does, he slows so much
that I take to sketching Baltimore skies.

We're far from home. Baltimore is a dream,
or Marrakech is a dream, or these mountains
above Marrakech where I've learned to say
star and stars, sun, rain, hello and thank you,

thank God—it's a dream. My dad stumbles up
stairs, as if just waking, but his eyes are staring.
When it starts to happen, we're still downstairs eating,
and as it's still happening, I learn from my dad

the difference between the words
for stroke and for heart attack, as I waste
more time reading about stroke symptoms.
The rhythm of relations fails too:

when I tell my sister in the other room
that our dad has had a heart attack,
she says, Does he really hate it here this much?
My mom says if I had only been at dinner earlier,

and I say nothing but I'm thinking
of the smell, which conjures to me
my grandmother's home and hospital rooms.
We wait all night for the car to arrive,

then drive seven hours back to the hotel.
My dad tries to stand from the lobby couch,
and stumbles blindly, still clutching his laptop
when the bellboys reseat him. Two of three

major coronary arteries blocked,
he's finally taken to a clinic.
While we're waiting, Djemaa El-Fna fills up
and empties three times.

Rupture: 1969 | 2021 | 1984 | 1996 | —

My mother is fifteen eating frozen buns
under a gaping sky dreaming of Shanghai
her mother & littlest brother crying
in private In my mother's mind
there is purpose to turning over dirt
to her body dragging across the border
slicing wheat hungry over the limbs
of the girl who trips & doesn't get up
she is tossed into the chasm
My mother dreams of war against bad men
the Soviets or Japanese
or so I imagine any chance to fill
the maw of her potential She wards off dreams
tap tapping on wood until it splinters inside

"农村也是大学"

"The countryside is also a university"

— PRC propaganda slogan

In total, approximately 17 million youth were exiled to rural areas in the 60s and 70s as a result of the Down to the Countryside movement.

April 2021

In China, family members gathered to celebrate what should have been Xiaojie Tan's 50th birthday two days after she was murdered in Atlanta. Tan's mother had not been told of her daughter's death because family members were worried it would make her sick.

Inside her dendritic branches reach
into the recesses of her mind misfiring
It is all neurofibrillary tangle
the past flaring up into the present
symptom of disease On her phone
my mother learns everything is rumor
hate is racially motivated or not
even as she loses the thread
I am trying to fill in the gaps
who was the girl who fell in the cracked
earth it slides into the present
into cracked volcanic plaque underneath
my sister My mother still remembers
her eldest lives on an island an ocean away

Oceans away I do not exist   yet
My mother   is used to losing faces
no longer young   but young enough to carry water
across the 弄堂   the last time
she sees her father-in-law   says goodbye
to her mother brothers   uncles aunties
neighbors teachers   It is the last time
she sees her baby brother   alive
She checks her pocket   for what she's forgetting
papers passport   twenty American dollars
the face of her small daughter   getting smaller
One year later   my sister follows
flying alone with a plastic tea set   sticky
towards a memory of her   mother

"After supper, the Master dismissed all except Sun Wukong, Zhu Bajie, and Sha the Monk. He took them out with him and said,

Look at that wonderful moonlight. It makes me long for the time when I can return home."
— *Wu Cheng'en,* Journey to the West

"Here, you see, it takes all the running you can do, to keep in the same place. If you want to get somewhere else, you must run at least twice as fast as that!"
— *Lewis Carroll,* Through the Looking Glass

I'm getting smaller   my mother's disease makes me
a child again   practicing handwriting
in the back of her store   chirping in English
Video Wonderland   *how can I help you*
hiding from adults so they can rent pornos though
one regular calls me China doll says I look just like
the Playboy bunny   in my third grade
Halloween costume   grins at my mother *tell me*
do all Asians   *sound the same in bed*
On a slow day   glass splinters over the register
just cash handed over   just ten years
away from her mother   fading alone in Shanghai
My mother alone   opens 9am the next day
the memory of the gun gaping   fresh in her mind

Mouths gape   open in the wet market
squirming & abundant   a full fish eel shrimp
the smell of what's alive   for now
Faces at the table   her brother & his
beautiful brain   without rupture
her father leaving   his mysterious anger
her sons still   born between me & my sister
& we're all hungry   for her mother's cooking
on the table   for nothing more than what we have
that moment   a synapse fires
& my mother remembers   she's taken us
with her already   all our faces
to this promise of a place   so free
we can do anything but   disappear

The Arrival

Where was I? The dark violet and green
velour couch, shrink-wrapped
night sky, streaked in 90's jazz, up-
holstered—in my parents' bedroom
it arrived. Out of context,
my friend Anne says, *It looks like nothing*,
about the sad stretch of houses
on our South Carolina trip, washed-out
flowerbushes speeding past.
The same hydrangeas lined up before
my first porch, where she sat: blue
dress, green lawn, family
on the other side of the world.
I am the same age now as she was then.
How can I say how it feels
to arrive? I draw lines across
the stiff fibers. I stroke
a soft and frivolous thing.

Legacy

"I used to love sweets," she says. "When you were little, I craved those sidewalk popsicles we bought for you."

Once you take food
from someone who's hungry,
what can you give them
in return? I thought that was
the story of Persephone, bound
to Hades on one side,
her mother on the other.

I wanted my father's calligraphy on the wall in my dorm. He wrote, "随遇而安."
Whatever happens, happens.

There is no such thing
as a stepping stone. Steps
fall away as you take them.
I never bought the idea of *nostos*,
Odysseus finding himself after
the long journey—what,
home?

Old Dogs (*Remember*)

You've heard the saying. The first day at home,
snub-nosed and sweet, house-trained but otherwise
unbroken, our rescue ignored every trick
in the book—classic commands: sit, stay,
be good, I begged. But as the wisdom goes:
At some point, learning comes too late. The sun
sinks on the dull glare of what used to cut,
bitter and sweet and just out of reach
of memory. Redemption is for those
who remember, and my mother slaps the glasses
off my father's face, laughing, her sharp edges
blunted into the barking violence of a bully.
Be good holds no water when the night falls,
dripping with the echo of another
she can't recall. The sound of time running out
sounds a lot like the word they keep asking her,
sounds like something she can almost string
together. Sounds, a little bit, like *surrender*.

Sick Days: Sonnet Corona

February 2023, Cambridge, Mass.

How many famous people have been sick
in this house? Famous meaning old. Horace
Mann had tuberculosis here, when cobalt
was thought to be the cure for consumption.

The day I got sick, I was at the doctor's,
but not in that order. Just the standard questions:
Family history of cancer? *I don't know*, I say, *we think so?*
Do I mention the lack of physicians in Cultural

Revolution–era China? She doesn't need a history lesson.
None, writes my doctor, and I think I should have given
the history lesson. Sex with men, women? *Anyone*, I say,
and at least that gets me a laugh, though I wasn't trying

to be funny. It's funny. I like to joke about the ghosts,
but they haven't shown up, yet.

I like to joke about the ghosts but
they haven't shown up yet and now
would be a good time. On a trip to Shanghai
to bury my grandmother, I went sightseeing

in the renovated 豫 garden, manufactured rockeries
and a zigzag bridge my uncle explained
gives you an advantage in outrunning
a goose. Only months later, writing

and rewriting the scene, I think that he probably
meant ghost. But outside, a goose startles and lurches
on the banks of the Charles, and the students shriek
from its hiss. Sometimes they must not be fast enough.

Maybe that is what my uncle meant.
What kind of creature can't navigate a turn?

What kind of creature can't navigate a turn?
I'm done sweating through the sheets. I've moved on
to pacing the room. Horrible things
probably happened here. When my sister calls,

I act worse than I am so I can get back
to reading aloud the dead poets. Someone wrote
a famous song about a meatball in this house. I play it.
I spill tea on Roget's *Third*, the first time

I'm cracking open the pages, and it's to put Kleenex
between them. It's a used copy so at least someone
has cracked the pages before. In my attic room,
there used to be an observatory, the only one in town.

The thing about stars is you can admire them in peace,
knowing they're already dead.

The thing about stars is you can admire them in peace,
knowing they're already dead. A physician in the 1800s,
Roget would have been familiar with the kingdom *mortis*.
He's famous now for classifying language, imposing rigor

on an undiagnosed mass of related words, his thesaurus.
I don't know if that has any bearing on his skill
as a physician, but I suppose I can relate, not hoping
to be remembered as a lawyer. I suppose I don't hope

to be remembered, period, but if it has to be for something,
I hope it's for a meatball song. I hope it's among friends.
I hope I was a good friend. There's a word that means
linger with me after the meal is done. I linger

and malinger. From the couch, I hear
my email ping. Everything on earth is busy.

Everything on earth is busy!
In 16th-century Shanghai, a son failed
his imperial exams and built a garden
in a show of filial piety. He called it 豫,

pleasing and satisfying to one's parents.
Diaries from the time mention it frequently
as the center of high society; in the shrubbery
red squirrels scampered and chirped. Next

the garden's upkeep ruined his family.
The moral of this story is that some people
have journaled for centuries, and I balk
at the idea of morning pages. Shanghainese

squirrels scurry. I wish I could drag each day
behind me like a weighted blanket.

I wish I could drag each day
behind me like a weighted blanket. But
in the yard, one tiny rabbit leaps over
another and newly leafed branches slash

at my windows. I'm afraid of what it means
to be left behind. To prepare for future
orientations, the law firm wants to know:
If you could have dinner

with any four people, dead or alive,
who with—and why? I live with four
of my very good friends, but godspeed
to anyone trying to schedule a full house.

I'll take what I can get. Anyone
who survives this is lucky.

Anyone who survives this is lucky.
What's a word the opposite of
unscathed? At a party before the pandemic,
a doctor-to-be tells me that we (society)

overinvest in the final years of life.
How do you know they're final? I want to say
but don't—I don't want him
to know I'm still listening. It's 2023.

The doctor-to-be is a doctor. Everything
that isn't terminal is chronic, and no one
is saying it's an emergency. It's not
too late. Emergency. *Emergency.* Am I lying

when I say I don't want to last forever,
not even in a poem?

I don't want to last forever, not even in a poem.
Would it be worse never to remember, or never
to forget? My mom says she can tell we're all waiting
for her to die, so to spite us, she's staying alive—

if she can remember to, ha ha. But spite is a feeling
that outlasts, so I'm sure she'll follow through.
I'm the keeper of her life's more sordid details
until I'm gone, too: meat cleaver crashing through

my bedroom door, broken leg at the foot of the stairs
all night, friends my friends—thirteen, all of us—sweeping
up the shattered plates. How did she get away with it?
How did they, the men who came to haunt us in her sleep,

get away each day without remembering
it? Who are you responsible for keeping alive?

Who are you responsible for keeping alive?
My mom asks me for the 500th time
if the St. Ives apricot scrub I bought her
is the same as her discontinued dollar store brand.

She likes to stare into the passenger seat mirror
while I drive. It's amazing that one of the final things
to leave her is her vanity. How do I know it's final?
On my last day in quarantine, I sat on the counter

and photographed myself for no one. For the internet,
I posted a black-and-white family photo, stiff postures
and plain Communist garb. Friends commented that they could see
an echo of her in me. My mother was beautiful and likes to pretend

that's all she was. She was. I wish I knew her
in the past tense. How many stars have been sick in this house?

How many people have walked
through these walls? I joke
about the ghosts when
they haven't said a word to me.

I don't know what I should be
running from. The stars, I understand,
are already dead. But everything
on earth is busy busy, and each day

passes me with me. I'm such a drag.
Wait. I mean I'm lucky. I know
I'm dying when I say I don't want to last
forever, buried in some poem.

Who made me
responsible for anything.

II

Privacy Policy

When you sign up for this slipstream, you give us certain information voluntarily. This includes your true name, legal name, username, the name you will give your first plant, your coordinates the first time you describe a meme in real life, the timestamp from the picture of your friend of a friend's 48th-percentile baby, the chat transcript with the undangerous stranger you told everything to at 13 (undangerous, it turns out, to you), the number of an emergency contact you broke up with five years ago; every time you've identified a crosswalk, jumble of letters, or nuclear power plant to verify your humanity; the results of 17 IQ tests you hope are wrong, the results of the Rorschach indicating your emotional stability is elite among those who have chosen to interpret inkblots online, your favorite Taco Bell menu item—discontinued but mentioned once on the annals of the plant forum where you post photos of your BOP (*Strelitzia reginae*) and await the glowing replies that will lead, in 42 clicks, off the edge of a flat earth.

you you
you
you
you
you you
you
you
await the glowing earth.

Big History

no need to be smug about your real sunlight
only with my eyes closed can I still remember it
burning my lids—it was glaring the day you
handed me the letter the paper was warm I
was doomed orange orange orange the only light
around me now extinguishes without fusion
what am I missing

what am I missing

I don't need to know that to know that was life—
so is this

Omens

Across the street, a man ran by, arms full
of shallots. I packed my partner's freezer full.
I can show love. I bought frozen tortellini
at the specialty foods store, trying not to listen

as the shop owner worried about running
out of goods. I went for a distanced walk, but while
I was out, my partner emptied the fridge, so unaware
of what we possessed—he thought it might all be

expired. I wish I weren't such a glutton for meaning.
Another poet might write about chance. By chance
we met on this very street, the night after I noticed
this stained-glass building, thought, *What kind of life*

is in there? By chance this virus replicated its strands
in some wet body that looked like mine. By chance, the color
of the light. Under which you might catch yourself,
villainous, benevolent, redeemed either way by your particular

dice roll. But then it was a seventeenth year and the cicadas
erupted. One hundred years ago, another flu. Friends'
parents have always died. There is an order to things.
Omens in the frozen goods. You can see them too.

The Reason

Branches partition the sky
each night I set shadows skittering
their small bodies in the under
brush and above me one brilliant eye
regards me no no many eyes regard me else
why skitter I'm the reason
for their flight from the groomed hedge
            I never get a moment alone

Headlights tremble because they
are hiding the humans hurtling
by in their machines there is sometimes
a baby in the machine capable of
nothing except its next meal biting
the cheek of the preferred mother but
any wire monkey could do
            Let's be "ourselves" right up to the end

I was circling the block pretending
we were a tragedy and then we were
so something out there must be listening
it's embarrassing to be caught pretending
but from where I stand Star Market is brighter
than both the moon and the sun rising now
ushering another sane day well time's healing
            Is that yesterday's rain

the algorithm moves toward an average

every day i prove my humanity to robots
every day i check my accounts
i listen to the children outside my window
                                        and am a child again
                                        listening to the other children
                                        outside the window
i felt from that experience then: i am one
of the species but not one with
every one feels this   unraveling
every one of us gets closer to

The trees are senescing, not dying. You're dying.

Has anyone been here long enough to love it?
Thirty-three years, and some days repeat already.
I come home and the mailbox is full again:

new credit cards promise liquidity, deals
I'll love, do not discard me, hello neighbor,
has anyone been here long enough to love it?

On the train, I catch a rectangle of light
that moves like childhood. Branches quake outside
my first home. Even there, the mailbox is full again.

The paper says our presidents are so old
their deaths wouldn't be a tragedy.
Has anyone been here long enough to love it?

How do you find the questions *before*
there are consequences to not answering them?
I come home and the mailbox is full again.

Everyone is full of it. I live with the consequences
of not answering them. Has anyone been here long
enough to love it? I come home and
I'm full and I'm full and I'm full.

Sestina

In 2011, I made a mistake.
Didn't understand what catastrophe was.
Studying in Paris, I didn't know
the difference between *l'amour* and *la mort*.
I thought tyranny was fashionable black
clothing. I couldn't pronounce moral desert.

People talk about what we deserve,
but that's probably a mistake.
Everything that *is* depends on what *was*—
call that an excuse, I know.
But in the end all that awaits is *la mort*.
My heart, my mother says, is black black black.

I have some courage but lack
the character to appreciate what life serves
when it serves shit. I've made mistakes.
I've loved the moon, especially when it was
on the water, shining on my potluck. But I know
everything runs its course. There it is. *La mort*.

Coeur, corps, cours, la mort, et l'amour.
At first I too tried to wear all black,
but in Morocco the desert
told me it was a mistake.
There's no use holding onto what was.
Every generation improves on another, I know

there was so much we didn't yet know.
Protests began that spring, more,
swelling. The sky was black.
I thought I was part of the desert.
As usual, I had no idea of the stakes—
just felt like I was expanding. I was.

Everyone loves to talk about what was
like what was was better. Maybe it was better, I don't know.
Or now is better, but it's also the end. *La Mort*,
next mass extinction, books burned black,
no one to read them. Just deserts.
Are those the right stakes?

Your hair on my pillow that winter was black.

After

I can look most things dead
on. In the dream, I lose
everyone. The houseplants yellow
in the tub while I run out
of air in the bedroom.
Their stalks wither after

the humidifier sputters after
days of drought. Are they dead?
Or is there more to lose
if I keep letting things go—yellow
to brown to too late to back out
of a bad deal now. Bathroom to bedroom

to bathroom to bedroom.
Don't say I avoid the inevitable after.
I confront my dread.
I eat until my body hangs loose.
The hands in my lap are otherworldly, yellow
in the artificial light. Looking in from out

there, a stranger thinks he's missing out
on warmth—my glowing bedroom
curated for love? Is that what I'm after?
The stranger's vision of the life I've led
in which I still have everything to lose?
The traffic light turns yellow,

and again a car speeds to catch that yellow
before it's red. A noise comes out
—of my mouth?—or outside my bedroom.
Some commotion after.
See? Life goes on no matter who's dead.
Strangers everywhere lose their lives, I lose

track of days, losses,
leaves, leavings, brown, yellow,
black rot in my tub. I still haven't gone out.
Someone in China owns this bedroom
I rent. Someone else will occupy it after.
The terms of the contract are never dead.

In the window, always, a vase of fresh-cut yellow flowers.

You tell me what comes after.

Refractory Period

I listen to a robot pronounce *coitus*
in three accents, to prepare for
a class on the history of marriage.
Nothing kills the mood faster

than terminology. *What's on your mind?*
M asks me after. Sometimes
it's tedious to be a social
animal. A class on the laws of

marriage is a class on the story of
disgust, which I learn is sometimes
justified and sometimes not. Which
is this? I tell M I'm thinking of mnemonic

arbitrage. It's not romantic but
it's more romantic than saying
that sex with M has reminded me
of sex: clicking teeth, smooth

obstruction, fingers catching—
what. Has my body been this strange
before? I could guess what we might do
to one another. When I want to transform

distance into tenderness, I imagine my subject
listening for their name in classroom attendance.
I can hear them calling *present*. Which reminds me
of the nostalgia in old photographs

of legendary despots: still boys and already
the world we might have known is gone.

Matter

I understand why some people believe, you say, yearning your head out the driver's seat window, car swerving beneath the screaming stars. The moon is the sun and the clouds roll through me. I don't want to be a part of your beautiful life.

Heart

Hours & hours
& hours & hour
s & hours & hou
rs & hours & h
ours & how will I
survive the hours
you've left

Ordinary Trouble

By the third stanza it's easy to forget
why I started this poem. So I abandon it.
Today's news sequence looks like
yesterday's. There's nothing to write
home about: Love is love? Big ideas
are a sleight of hand, untroubled

by an after. I'm healthily troubled,
according to my therapist. It's natural to forget,
Holly says, that spring can feel like the end of it:
drunk bees flowering like last time, like
it's the last time. The deranged bees have it right.
When it comes, the end will appear as another bright idea,

not an emergency exit. My worst ideas
don't get much air in therapy, where my trouble
comes from realizing what I want to forget
has a life of its own. Not every poem can be a hit.
What you recall isn't what it was like.
There's violence, too, in getting it right

most of the time. I'm done trying to be right
most of the time. The marketplace of ideas
inflates whenever I check on it. Trouble
still finds me, finds me though I swear to forget
it, swear not to know what I know, swear it
was a different poem where I acted like

there was an order to things, wrote it like
you too could see it. Like a writer
in seasonal disorder, every idea
is hollow if you're in deep enough. There's trouble
and then there's trouble. I forget
if seasonal means every season in this climate.

I wish I could put my finger on the it of it—
the reason I started this poem. Reader, I like you. Like
you, there are times I think I'm mostly right.
I find my mistakes in the repetition, ideas
worn in the mind by rhyme. You're troubled
for a moment by its echo. Then you forget.

Relational, or Instructions for Going On

Once you realize it's possible to stop
in the middle of anything then

In Boston, my roommate Nadia watches
videos of strangers getting ready for bed:
brushing their teeth, taking out contacts,
removing makeup. Sometimes a candle
is involved. Some self-care ritual to handle
the passage of time. The dripping wax
on my table doesn't pool so much as spread
satisfyingly into a seal that cools as I watch.

*

This is as good a place as any to stop. I forget
what it's like to be new in a city until
I feel someone new to me see it
through my eyes. Broadway, a street

I've walked down a million times, in a million
states, open-hearted, dazed, professionally attired
and puking in that trash can, crossing the street
to dodge an ill-timed friend, keeping my distance

to keep strangers safe. There never stop being
so many unknowns. The word *home* lodges
in the throat, and familiar rituals blip before
my eyes, like a life. I buy overpriced fruit.

In the park, dogs picnic in the late afternoon light.
This place as easy as any to forget.

*

In the afternoon it's easy to forget what is
is. The light coming through the curtains coming
from another time. When I was seven, I visited Shanghai,
and thought, afterwards, that I missed it. I thought

that place was mine to miss. Cigarette smoke after
reminded me of my uncles, reminded me that uncles
existed, in some version of home where no one
expected us back.

Embarrassingly, I called it mine.

*

Over Boston, I watch the coastline
curve out of sight. In the water,
the ripple of a boat. Otherwise tranquil
open skies. I have no fear of flying.

At my first job after college, I taught
fourth graders in another country. Clueless,
I tried to read them Auden: *About suffering*
they were never wrong...What

about suffering? We spent the entire lesson
on that line. Someone's sister is in the hospital now.
My plane is headed for Baltimore where my mother
has taken a fall. After Baltimore, the plane stops

in Chicago, Sacramento. Deadlines,
scheduled flights, and some people move on.

*

me, to my mother: *you have to let others be*
her response to me: *but you're not an other*

*

Dread, among other things, makes me angry.
I don't know if it's the inevitable I dread so much as
seeing it. The body slumped. The moment of panic.
Or, maybe worse, not panic but reluctance. I don't feel

enough. At first not realizing what's going on, saying
something in annoyance, like *sit up*, pulling the chair
out, the thud. If I see it clearly enough, do I still
have to undergo it? I know now that not everyone

moves on. The moment after which I'll be alone alone
alone

*

How to stop. I've made it sound easy but the lights keep changing just as we reach them at crosswalks where we open to the unknown should the unknown choose us. Mistakes were made and some of them are mine. There is just enough time now to miss it.

Sometimes you have to be still and suffer,

my teacher says about writing, but I
have an active suffering that calls me
to run after it. *Keep up*, says the feed
of bad news. It's dangerous to see others

as an abstraction. I don't need to hate anyone
as an abstraction because I have my mother—I hate
my mother. She who keeps stealing the car keys
is very real. I see her; I know Terror. What does it mean

that I know just where to find a sugar baby but not
a nice companion for my Terror? What does it say
about me that I'd rather be a sugar baby than a nice
companion for my mother? I don't actually

know if that's true. But when I'm in a car chasing
my mother down I-95, wind slicing through the papers
in the backseat, I'm not thinking about writing,
or about suffering, even if that's what this is.

Convergence

I. Glitch

Not quite morning, something whirs at my side
& I smack the phone but it doesn't stop
the twittering coming through the window
like dial-up. My real alarm (*early_twilight.mp3*)
is an ascendancy of cricket sounds
over the swamp of a dream
in which the spaceship finally delivers us
underwater. The twittering
slams into the window. Another casualty
of the bugs crawling the system, looping through
a function defined as lawn care
& the study of death.

II. Invention

Filaments pulse light across oceans
so that I can watch a rocket landing
through a surface purer
than filtered water. The secret of glass:
purified ash transformed
from something to look at
into something to look through:
when *indivisible* became *individual*
in the frame of a mirror and the mirror
reflected our collective destiny: the flag
planted in space, the cities glittering
across what once was cosmically dark, the first time
you looked up at the blurry borders, the light
/dark shapes of your mother's face, and thought
Mine.

III. Machine Learning

The first time the machine posed a question,
we thought of our children. We thought
Curiosity, Spirit, Perseverance. We thought
growth mindset. My mother turns to me
to ask why the sky looks like rain & when
her mother is coming home, not
for the first time. In the grass below my window,
a small pile of feathers & filaments
curves into itself. We learn
this final position.

III

Insomnia

Refuse the day.
In the night,

a jewel balloon will hang

doubled in the snow,
an echo like anger

curled in the mind,
like a peeled thing

without eyes, troubled,
finite, and proud.

Like the living.
Now light rushes in

from the window,

flooding the day
before you.

嫦娥 (The Moon Lady)

My shadow stains the moon. Will I return to Earth?
Everything looks brighter here, but not as clear.

Everything looks brighter here, but not as clear:
A million compromises crowd our Earth.

I've made a million compromises since birth:
When I was a girl, I was the last to eat.

I was still just a girl—I longed to eat
Treats baked at dawn with egg yolk, lotus, red bean,

Your mooncakes split at dusk with lotus filling.
The elixir of life wasn't nearly so sweet.

The elixir of life went quickly, my sweet—
I betrayed you, drank it all,

I drank it all down. My betrayal
Stains the moon. Will I return to Earth?

Turbulence

The moon just visible
in the still-blue sky looks over another
unfamiliar city. Like everything I imagine
it's yours. The drunken lurch

of this made thing, constructed
like the world beneath it: neat
green rows, hot polymer rooftops,
sidewalks surrounding hedges

lining driveways glittered
with cars. Beyond lit windows
forks and knives are placed
like their people. It is a life.

We've made it. In the sky
I want to call somebody still
new to me, to tell them
what I've just seen. It's impossible,

bigger than I'm allowed to say.

Intimacy

after Gu Cheng

Reader,
look at me—
then look at the clouds.
I feel you—
watching me, so remote.
Watching the clouds, so close.

Patina

He had Beethoven's ego but not his talent. Regardless

we could name both of them centuries later, Beethoven and
the other one. Who am I forgetting tonight?

Across the street, a warm light flicks
on between aged brick and copper. Imagine wanting

only what matters over time.

Love Poem for Brood X

Consider a moment
what the cicada knows—
take your time
growing in soil rich
with the bodies
that came before you.
Make the days last
until they're done. Stay
out of trouble
until you forget what you know
and long for the beginning: *remember*
how fresh the new world was?
Listen. Emerge
as swarm. Shed your first body
& sing, throw a party
as the last defense of your species.
It would be enough
to put on a good show,
to be the last thing They see
at the end, stumbling home:
two red eyes in the dark, dawning.

Final Frontier

A deer flew over the car & the stars blinked back their curse. In childhood it was all possible as the hours, and real. My wild bed turned in the dark until I could acknowledge everything shining, safe as I would ever be, asleep. Twenty years later, I wish at 11:11 on the same unlit roads, home for the last time & I remember it: the ritual counting of stars, the reality as strangling as myth, appeals to a world of wonders impossible to control.

On April 29th, I try to be in the world

Somewhere I read
that every second
the eye is exposed

the sun destructs
color and painters
must be wary of

the light. But spring
is green exploding
bright bright bright

Love Poem for My Friends on a Road Trip to the End of the World and Also the Beginning

The first skim of light dawning over I-95:
highway beach & cramped delight *& been too long*
the faces of my friends *how*
I love you in the timeless glow of a Taco Bell parking lot brimming
with the purple hours of radio talk & welcome
centers everything we know contained in one car
I think there must be nothing better
than the first shock of saltwater after
hatching in the sand getting lost
in the obsidian dark in the decade
of seasky in the peaceful eradication
of borders not these churning waters
melting ice *there is so much movement*
before the end ice melting
in our drinks & sandwiches
crumbling on the counter / the pop
hiss & faces of the ones we love
basking in the starlight of I mean
drinking in the mystery of
I mean to say living in witness of
one another in this world
we surrender

St. Augustine

On the lazy
river, the rain
fell harder. It was
frantic. And we were
the only four beings on the

water, unless—who suggested it?
crocodile bait—we shrieked even as
it became memory. Real fear
soaked through with real

delight. I don't want to say
what I think I'd suffer to
keep drifting on that
day as long as
I'm alive.

Mantis Marriage: A Fable

The grass blades scissor the sky with green,
cut clouds to pieces over insect dreams.

The female mantis—large, formidable—
approaches, clicking savage mandibles.

She searches for a husband in the grass,
an arthropod worth mating with—alas

when soon she spots the male's pathetic frame
with flimsy bamboo wings exposed and lame,

she can't profess he's swept her off her tarsus,
but still the sex might lead to some catharsis.

She grazes whiskers over and behind
his temples—he and she are intertwined—

he clasps two legs together now and prays.
The autumn afternoon draws back its rays.

The forest trembles as the wind grows cold,
the evening colors, lovers limbs unfold.

She turns as if to give a final kiss,
swiftly crunches his skull. Could there exist

another pair as faithful unto death
as they who consummate with dying breath?

梁祝 (The Butterfly Lovers)

they spent the summer spinning
silk buttons fastened
in air. he found her humming
to swaying leaves. a current
across persuasions
blew until the world quaked,
and split form—
and the bodies at stake,
the interior paramour,
the pupae inside the chrysalides,
evolved, became exterior:
extended wings studded with the Pleiades.
a pulse quickens before it slows.
from one death in the dark, they eclose.

Glossolalia

It starts when something falls
into me. A pale moth lands
on the steps of the chapel
in a wine-tinged shadow—mute
fur trembling. I am of course

"uncomfortable."

There comes a time, you say,
in faith, when one allows oneself
to speak in tongues. Under the light
your steady hand lifts above
two ruined wings, fluttering.

The Thing About Paradise

is that it's full of the recently deceased:
scattered feathers, still writhing tails, compost
for the orchard teeming with life.

Appendix

In the catalog of Days, I can identify all the moments I was in love. Like Day 67 of 15,809 with N—I looked at him in a cold sweat, after he said, *Try the live octopus,* and only after the tentacle squiggled into my mouth, and I tasted nothing but pure predatory instinct like fear, back-of-the-throat sour, only after I began to swallow, N said, *Make sure you chew thoroughly, or it might stick.* I wanted to throttle him on Day 67 and didn't. Or Days 807 to 13,009, when I forgot to be embarrassed by my own vanity, sitting in the bathroom sink peeling my nails and talking about my day—or was that not 807 to 13,009? I thought the index for *Lovers,*

N, see also *Love letters;*
First readers; Pork bone
soup

ended at 15,809 (see *Regrettable behavior*) but—last week, something shifted in the window of our old apartment, and there it all was: still lit, still.

A Guide to Seed Propagation in Hawai'i

I wish I could tell you to wait for something
hardy and easy to grow, like the jungle
ginger twining underfoot—or promise
that the unexpected journey will take root,
like the seed traveling three thousand miles
in a lost bird—*T. persecutrix, persecutus*—banished
to a paradise in the nowhere of the world,
vines prostrate and sprawling,

please

I can't ask you to wait
but know that it could be worth it
like the ripe fruit falling off
into your hands, when it's ready.

Slipstream

The guide says to let my body be quiet and now I can't stop. I've been quiet on my couch for five hours. I was quiet a long time on the floor where I took off my shoes. Now I'm in the room. You called, and I silenced the phone. This quiet isn't about you. In a list of deaths I don't have to choose, I choose anyway. Bury myself in quietude. Things pile up. Actually, the quiet in me is like the quiet in you. I think I'm looking for the word still.

ACKNOWLEDGMENTS

A number of the poems in this collection were first published elsewhere, sometimes in slightly different forms. Grateful acknowledgment is made to the following journals, their editors, and publishers:

"Sometimes you have to be still and suffer" *The Yale Review*, Poem of the Week, January 2025

"Privacy Policy" *Taco Bell Quarterly*, Issue 7, October 2024

"Laundry, Clean Room, Shower, Trash Day, Taxes", "Relational", & "The Reason" *diode*, Spring 2025

"Every Day the World," "A Guide to Seed Propagation in Hawai'i," & "The Thing About Paradise" *The Georgia Review*, Winter 2022

"Convergence" & "Old Dogs (*Remember*)" *Crazyhorse* (now *swamp pink*), Issue 100, Fall 2021

"Moon Lady" & "Butterfly Lovers" *Ecotone*, Issue 30, Spring/Summer 2021

"Love Poem for Brood X" *32 Poems*, Issue 40, Fall/Winter 2022

"Rupture: 1969 | 2021 | 1984 | 1996 | —" *Hayden's Ferry Review*, Issue 69, Spring 2022

"Glossolalia" & "Appendix" *Gulf Coast*, Issue 34.1 Winter/Spring 2022

"Sick Days: Sonnet Corona" *Nimrod International Journal*, Vol 67, No. 1, Fall/Winter 2023

"love poem for the middle of love" *The Journal*, Issue 46.2, Summer 2021

"Final Frontier", "Hi, I'm sorry to keep missing you," & "Insomnia" *HAD* Fall 2023, Summer 2024, & Fall 2025

"Omens," "Ordinary Trouble," & "love poem for my friends on a road trip to the end of the world and also the beginning" *Sixth Finch* Fall 2022, Winter 2024

"The Arrival" *Poet Tree*, Issue 1, Summer 2024

"Big History," "After," & "Patina" *Waxwing*, Fall 2025

"the algorithm moves toward an average" & "Refractory Period" *dialogist*, January 2025

RECENT & SELECTED TITLES FROM TUPELO PRESS

of Women: Twenty Japanese Female Poets / 20 Waka Poems Naoko Fujimoto, editor & translator
Extinction Song John James
The Book of Marys and Glaciers Carrie Olivia Adams
The Andrew Wyeth Chronicles Janée Baugher
Identifying the Pathogen Jennifer Militello
Other Paths for Shahrazad: A Bilingual Anthology of Contemporary Poetry by Arab Women Jennifer Jean, editor
Indifferent Cities Ángel García
Open House: Conversations with Writers about Community Kristina Marie Darling, editor
Something Small of How to See a River Teresa Dzieglewicz
Force Drift: An Essay in the Epic Jeffrey Pethybridge
Tips to Help You Do Your Best Mike Carlson
Cyborg Fever Laurie Sheck
Daphne Kristen Case
Nebulous Vertigo Belle Ling
Westminster West Chard de Niord
Jalousie Allyson Paty
Mycocosmic Lesley Wheeler
Phantom Number: An Abecedarium for April Spring Ulmer
The Last Milkweed Alan Berolzheimer, Jeffrey Levine, & Allison O'Keefe, eds.
The Haunting Cate Peebles
The Radiant Lise Goett
The Opening Ritual G.C. Waldrep
The Right Hand Christina Pugh
Called Back Rosa Lane
Landsickness Leigh Lucas
Green Island Liz Countryman
The Beautiful Immunity Karen An-hwei Lee
Small Altars Justin Gardiner
Country Songs for Alice Emma Binder
Asterism Ae Hee Lee
then telling be the antidote Xiao Yue Shan
Therapon Bruce Bond & Dan Beachy-Quick
membery Preeti Kaur Rajpal
How To Live Kelle Groom
Sleep Tight Satellite Carol Guess
THINE Kate Partridge
The Future Will Call You Something Else Natasha Sajé
Night Logic Matthew Gellman
The Unreal City Mike Lala
Wind—Mountain—Oak: Poems of Sappho Dan Beachy-Quick
Tender Machines J. Mae Barizo
Best of Tupelo Quarterly Kristina Marie Darling, Ed.
We Are Changed to Deer at the Broken Place Kelly Weber
Why Misread a Cloud Emily Carlson
The Strings Are Lightning and Hold You In Chee Brossy
Ore Choir: The Lava on Iceland Katy Didden, Kevin Tsang illustration
The Air in the Air Behind It Brandon Rushton
The Future Perfect: A Fugue Eric Pankey
American Massif Nicholas Regiacorte
City Scattered Tyler Mills
Today in the Taxi Sean Singer
April at the Ruins Lawrence Raab